The Psychology Behind Effective Copywriting

KHAIRUL HILMI SIDEK

Copyright © 2024 KHAIRUL HILMI SIDEK

All rights reserved

The characters and events portrayed in this book are fictitious. Any similarity to real persons, living or dead, is coincidental and not intended by the author.

No part of this book may be reproduced, or stored in a retrieval system, or transmitted in any form or by any means, electronic, mechanical, photocopying, recording, or otherwise, without express written permission of the publisher.

Contents

Title Page

Copyright

Chapter 1: The Importance of Psychology in Copywriting — 1

Chapter 2: Overview of Psychological Triggers and Techniques — 4

Chapter 3: What are Psychological Triggers? — 7

Chapter 4: How Psychological Triggers Affect Consumer Behavior — 11

Chapter 5: The Role of Emotional Resonance in Copywriting — 15

Chapter 6: How to Tap into Cognitive Biases to Craft Compelling Copy — 19

Chapter 7: Psychological Techniques to Enhance Your Copy — 23

Chapter 8: Understanding Your Audience — 27

Chapter 9: Crafting a Strong Value Proposition — 31

Chapter 10: The Role of Storytelling in Copywriting — 35

Chapter 11: Creating Urgency and Scarcity in Your Copy — 39

Chapter 12: The Impact of Visual Elements in Copywriting — 42

Chapter 13: Crafting Effective Calls to Action (CTAs) — 46

Chapter 14: Leveraging Social Proof in Copywriting — 50

Chapter 15: The Importance of Consistency in Copywriting — 54

Chapter 16: Using Humor in Copywriting — 58

Chapter 17: Ethical Copywriting — 62

Chapter 18: The Psychology of Color in Copywriting 66
Chapter 19: The Importance of Typography in Copywriting 70
Chapter 20: The Role of Layout and Design in Copywriting 74
Chapter 21: The Use of White Space in Copywriting 78
Chapter 22: The Role of Images and Graphics in Copywriting 82
Chapter 23: The Art of Writing Persuasive Headlines 86

Chapter 1: The Importance of Psychology in Copywriting

Understanding the Role of Psychology in Copywriting

Copywriting is more than just putting words on a page; it's about crafting messages that resonate with the audience and drive them to take action. At its core, effective copywriting taps into the psychological principles that influence human behavior. Understanding these principles allows copywriters to create content that not only captures attention but also compels the reader to act.

Why Psychology Matters

Psychology provides insights into how people think, feel, and make decisions. By leveraging psychological principles, copywriters can:

- **Enhance Persuasion:** Understanding what motivates people enables copywriters to craft messages that align with those motivations, making the copy more persuasive.
- **Build Trust:** Trust is a crucial element in any transaction. Psychological techniques can help establish and build trust with the audience.
- **Create Emotional Connections:** Emotions play a significant role in decision-making. Effective copy taps into the emotions of the audience, creating a deeper

connection with the brand or product.

- **Improve Engagement:** By understanding what captures attention and holds interest, copywriters can create more engaging content that keeps the audience reading.

Key Psychological Concepts in Copywriting

1. **Emotional Triggers:** Emotions drive actions. Identifying and leveraging the right emotional triggers can make copy more impactful.
2. **Cognitive Biases:** These are systematic patterns of deviation from norm or rationality in judgment. By understanding cognitive biases, copywriters can craft messages that align with these biases, making them more effective.
3. **Social Proof:** People tend to follow the actions of others. Incorporating social proof, such as testimonials or user reviews, can increase credibility and trust.
4. **Scarcity and Urgency:** The perception of scarcity or a limited-time offer can drive people to act quickly. This principle is often used in promotional copy to increase conversions.
5. **Reciprocity:** The principle of reciprocity suggests that people are more likely to return a favor. Providing value to the audience first can create a sense of obligation and increase the likelihood of a positive response.

The Science Behind Effective Copy

Research in psychology and behavioral economics provides a wealth of knowledge that can be applied to copywriting. Studies on attention, memory, and decision-making processes help us understand what makes certain messages more effective than others. For instance, the concept of "framing" suggests that the way information is presented (positive vs. negative framing) can significantly impact how it is perceived and acted upon.

Practical Applications

To apply psychological principles effectively, copywriters should:

- **Conduct Audience Research:** Understand the demographics, preferences, and behaviors of the target audience.
- **Test and Optimize:** Continuously test different approaches and optimize based on what works best for the audience.
- **Stay Ethical:** Use psychological techniques responsibly and avoid manipulation or deceit.

Conclusion

Understanding the psychology behind effective copywriting is essential for creating messages that resonate with the audience and drive action. By leveraging psychological principles, copywriters can enhance their persuasive power, build trust, and create emotional connections with their audience. This foundational knowledge sets the stage for the more detailed techniques and strategies covered in the subsequent chapters.

Chapter 2: Overview of Psychological Triggers and Techniques

Introduction to Psychological Triggers

Psychological triggers are cues that influence the mental and emotional state of an individual, leading them to take a specific action. In copywriting, understanding and utilizing these triggers can significantly enhance the effectiveness of your messages. These triggers are rooted in human psychology and can be leveraged to create compelling and persuasive copy.

Key Psychological Triggers

1. **Fear of Missing Out (FOMO):** People tend to act quickly when they fear losing an opportunity. Phrases like "limited time offer" or "only a few left" can create a sense of urgency.
2. **Curiosity:** Creating a sense of curiosity can draw readers in. Headlines or opening statements that hint at something interesting or valuable encourage people to keep reading.
3. **Social Proof:** As mentioned in Chapter 1, social proof leverages the tendency of people to follow the actions of others. Testimonials, reviews, and endorsements can build credibility and trust.
4. **Scarcity:** Like FOMO, the principle of scarcity suggests that people place higher value on things that are less

available. Limited editions or exclusive offers can drive action.

5. **Authority:** People tend to trust and follow the advice of experts. Incorporating quotes or endorsements from industry leaders can enhance the credibility of your copy.

6. **Reciprocity:** Offering something of value first, such as free information or a trial, can create a sense of obligation in the audience to reciprocate.

7. **Consistency and Commitment:** Once people commit to something, they are more likely to follow through. Encouraging small initial commitments can lead to larger actions over time.

Techniques for Leveraging Psychological Triggers

1. **Storytelling:** Stories are a powerful way to engage the audience and tap into their emotions. A well-crafted story can incorporate multiple psychological triggers, such as empathy, curiosity, and social proof.

2. **Personalization:** Tailoring your message to the individual can make it more relevant and engaging. Personalized greetings, recommendations, and offers can enhance the connection with the audience.

3. **Vivid Imagery:** Using descriptive language and visual elements can create mental images that resonate with the audience. This can enhance the emotional impact of your copy.

4. **Clear and Compelling Calls to Action (CTAs):** A strong CTA is essential for driving action. It should be clear, concise, and aligned with the psychological triggers in your copy.

5. **Positive Framing:** Presenting information in a positive light can make it more appealing. For example, highlighting benefits rather than avoiding losses can

be more persuasive.

Practical Examples

- **Fear of Missing Out (FOMO):** "Don't miss out on this exclusive offer! Only available for the next 24 hours."
- **Curiosity:** "Discover the secret to boosting your sales—read on to find out more."
- **Social Proof:** "Join thousands of satisfied customers who have transformed their businesses with our solution."
- **Scarcity:** "Limited edition—only 100 units available!"
- **Authority:** "According to industry experts, our product is the best solution for your needs."
- **Reciprocity:** "Get your free eBook today and learn the top strategies for success."
- **Consistency and Commitment:** "Start with our free trial and see the results for yourself."

Ethical Considerations

While psychological triggers can be powerful tools in copywriting, it's important to use them ethically. Manipulative or deceptive practices can damage your reputation and lead to long-term negative consequences. Always aim to provide genuine value and build trust with your audience.

Conclusion

Understanding and leveraging psychological triggers can significantly enhance the effectiveness of your copywriting. By tapping into the mental and emotional states of your audience, you can create compelling messages that drive action. In the following chapters, we'll delve deeper into specific psychological principles and techniques, providing you with a comprehensive toolkit for effective copywriting.

Chapter 3: What are Psychological Triggers?

Defining Psychological Triggers

Psychological triggers are stimuli that prompt individuals to take specific actions. These triggers tap into innate human behaviors and responses, influencing how people think, feel, and act. In the context of copywriting, understanding these triggers allows you to craft messages that resonate deeply with your audience, leading to higher engagement and conversion rates.

How Psychological Triggers Work

Psychological triggers operate by activating certain mental and emotional responses. When a trigger is effectively used in copywriting, it can lead to:

- **Increased Attention:** Triggers can capture the reader's attention and make them more likely to engage with the content.
- **Emotional Responses:** Triggers can evoke emotions, which play a critical role in decision-making.
- **Behavioral Changes:** Triggers can influence the reader's behavior, encouraging them to take the desired action.

Common Psychological Triggers

1. **Emotions:** Emotions like happiness, fear, anger, and

sadness can drive behavior. For example, a message that evokes fear can prompt the reader to take action to avoid a negative outcome.

2. **Cognitive Biases:** These are systematic patterns of deviation from norm or rationality in judgment. Examples include the confirmation bias, where people favor information that confirms their preconceptions, and the anchoring effect, where people rely heavily on the first piece of information they receive.

3. **Social Proof:** Seeing others take a particular action can encourage individuals to do the same. Testimonials, reviews, and user-generated content are powerful forms of social proof.

4. **Scarcity:** People are more likely to want something that is in limited supply. Limited time offers and exclusive deals create a sense of urgency and desire.

5. **Authority:** People tend to trust and follow the advice of experts or authoritative figures. Endorsements from credible sources can enhance the persuasiveness of your message.

6. **Reciprocity:** When people receive something of value, they feel a sense of obligation to return the favor. Offering free resources or helpful information can lead to increased goodwill and action.

7. **Consistency and Commitment:** Once individuals commit to something, they are more likely to follow through. Encouraging small, initial commitments can lead to larger actions over time.

Practical Applications in Copywriting

1. **Emotions:** Use storytelling to evoke emotions. For example, a story about a customer overcoming a challenge with your product can evoke empathy and inspire action.

2. **Cognitive Biases:** Use anchoring by presenting a high price first, followed by a lower price, to make the lower price seem more attractive.
3. **Social Proof:** Highlight user reviews and testimonials to build credibility and trust.
4. **Scarcity:** Create urgency with phrases like "Only a few left" or "Offer ends soon."
5. **Authority:** Include quotes or endorsements from experts to enhance credibility.
6. **Reciprocity:** Offer valuable content or free trials to build goodwill.
7. **Consistency and Commitment:** Start with small asks, such as signing up for a newsletter, before moving to larger requests, like purchasing a product.

Examples of Psychological Triggers in Action

- **Emotions:** "Imagine the relief you'll feel when you never have to worry about [problem] again."
- **Cognitive Biases:** "Most people choose our premium plan for just $99, but you can start with the basic plan for only $49."
- **Social Proof:** "Join over 10,000 satisfied customers who have transformed their lives with our program."
- **Scarcity:** "Hurry! Only 5 spots left for this exclusive event."
- **Authority:** "As recommended by leading industry experts, our solution is the best in the market."
- **Reciprocity:** "Download our free guide to learn the top strategies for success."
- **Consistency and Commitment:** "Start your journey today with our free trial. If you love it, you can upgrade to our premium plan."

Conclusion

Psychological triggers are powerful tools in copywriting, enabling you to create messages that resonate with your audience and drive action. By understanding and applying these triggers, you can enhance the effectiveness of your copy and achieve better results. In the next chapter, we will explore the role of emotional resonance in creating effective copy.

Chapter 4: How Psychological Triggers Affect Consumer Behavior

The Connection Between Psychology and Consumer Behavior

Consumer behavior is heavily influenced by psychological triggers. These triggers tap into the subconscious mind, affecting how people perceive information, make decisions, and ultimately act. By understanding these connections, copywriters can craft messages that align with the natural thought processes and behaviors of their audience.

Key Psychological Triggers and Their Impact on Behavior

1. **Emotional Triggers:** Emotions drive a significant portion of consumer behavior. When a message evokes strong emotions, whether positive or negative, it can lead to immediate action. For instance, fear can prompt people to avoid a perceived threat, while happiness can encourage them to pursue a positive outcome.
2. **Cognitive Biases:** These biases shape the way people interpret information. For example, the anchoring effect can influence purchasing decisions by setting a reference point. If the initial price presented is high, subsequent prices may seem more reasonable by comparison, even if they are still relatively high.
3. **Social Proof:** Seeing others engage in a behavior can

validate that behavior for an individual. This is why testimonials, reviews, and social media endorsements are powerful—they provide evidence that others have had positive experiences with a product or service.

4. **Scarcity:** The fear of missing out on a limited opportunity can prompt quick decisions. Limited-time offers, low stock warnings, and exclusive deals create a sense of urgency that drives consumers to act before they miss their chance.

5. **Authority:** Endorsements from credible sources can significantly impact consumer behavior. When an authority figure recommends a product, it lends credibility and trust, making consumers more likely to follow the recommendation.

6. **Reciprocity:** Offering something of value can create a sense of obligation in the consumer to reciprocate. Free trials, samples, and valuable content can lead to increased goodwill and a higher likelihood of conversion.

7. **Consistency and Commitment:** Once consumers commit to a small action, they are more likely to continue in the same direction. Therefore initial low-barrier actions, such as signing up for a newsletter, can lead to larger commitments, like making a purchase.

Examples of Psychological Triggers in Action

1. **Emotional Triggers:** A charity ad showing images of people in need can evoke sympathy and prompt donations.

2. **Cognitive Biases:** Retailers often display the original price alongside the sale price to emphasize the discount, leveraging the anchoring effect.

3. **Social Proof:** An online course website showing the number of students enrolled and their positive feedback can encourage new enrollments.

4. **Scarcity:** An e-commerce site displaying "Only 3 items left in stock!" can drive immediate purchases.
5. **Authority:** A toothpaste brand endorsed by dentists can influence consumers to choose that brand over others.
6. **Reciprocity:** A SaaS company offering a free eBook in exchange for an email address can build goodwill and lead to future sales.
7. **Consistency and Commitment:** A fitness app offering a free 7-day trial can lead to a paid subscription as users commit to their fitness goals.

Practical Tips for Using Psychological Triggers

1. **Know Your Audience:** Tailor your use of psychological triggers to the preferences and behaviors of your target audience.
2. **Create Emotional Appeals:** Use storytelling, vivid imagery, and relatable scenarios to evoke emotions in your audience.
3. **Leverage Social Proof:** Highlight testimonials, user reviews, and endorsements to build trust and credibility.
4. **Introduce Scarcity:** Use limited-time offers and low stock warnings to create a sense of urgency.
5. **Use Authority Figures:** Incorporate endorsements from credible experts or influencers to enhance the persuasiveness of your message.
6. **Offer Value First:** Provide free resources, trials, or samples to build goodwill and create a sense of obligation.
7. **Encourage Small Commitments:** Start with low-barrier actions to build momentum toward larger commitments.

Conclusion

Psychological triggers play a crucial role in shaping consumer behavior. By understanding and strategically applying these triggers, copywriters can create more effective and persuasive messages. In the next chapter, we will delve into the role of emotional resonance in crafting compelling copy.

Chapter 5: The Role of Emotional Resonance in Copywriting

Understanding Emotional Resonance

Emotional resonance refers to the ability of a message to evoke strong emotions in the audience. In copywriting, creating emotional resonance means crafting content that connects with readers on a deep, emotional level, making them more likely to engage with the message and act.

The Power of Emotions in Decision Making

Emotions play a critical role in decision making. Research shows that emotional responses often drive decisions, even more so than rational thought. When a piece of copy resonates emotionally, it can:

- **Capture Attention:** Emotional content stands out and is more likely to capture the reader's attention.
- **Create Memorable Impressions:** People are more likely to remember content that evokes strong emotions.
- **Drive Action:** Emotions can be powerful motivators, prompting readers to act based on how they feel.

Key Emotions to Evoke in Copywriting

1. **Happiness:** Messages that evoke happiness can create a positive association with the brand or product. This can lead to increased engagement and loyalty.
2. **Fear:** Fear can prompt immediate action to avoid a

negative outcome. This is often used in messages about safety, health, and security.

3. **Anger:** While potentially risky, evoking anger can motivate readers to take action against perceived injustices or problems.

4. **Sadness:** Sadness can evoke empathy and compassion, often leading to supportive actions such as donations or advocacy.

5. **Surprise:** Surprise can capture attention and make the message more memorable. It can also prompt curiosity and further engagement.

Techniques for Creating Emotional Resonance

1. **Storytelling:** Stories are a powerful way to evoke emotions. A well-told story can make the audience feel connected to the characters and the outcome.

2. **Visuals:** Images and videos can enhance the emotional impact of your message. Visuals that complement the emotional tone of your copy can make it more compelling.

3. **Descriptive Language:** Use vivid, descriptive language to paint a picture and evoke emotions. Words that appeal to the senses can make the content more engaging.

4. **Relatability:** Create content that reflects the experiences and emotions of your audience. When readers see themselves in your message, it can create a stronger emotional connection.

5. **Testimonials and Case Studies:** Real-life stories from customers can evoke emotions and provide social proof. These stories can show how your product or service has positively impacted others.

Examples of Emotional Resonance in Action

- **Happiness:** "Imagine the joy on your child's face when

they open their dream gift."
- **Fear:** "Don't let identity theft ruin your life. Protect yourself now with our advanced security solutions."
- **Anger:** "It's time to stand up against unfair practices. Join us in fighting for your rights."
- **Sadness:** "Every day, thousands go hungry. Your donation can make a difference."
- **Surprise:** "You won't believe what happened next! Discover the shocking truth."

Practical Tips for Crafting Emotionally Resonant Copy

1. **Know Your Audience:** Understand the emotions that resonate most with your target audience. Tailor your content to evoke these emotions.
2. **Be Authentic:** Authenticity is key to emotional resonance. Ensure that the emotions you evoke are genuine and align with your brand values.
3. **Balance Emotions:** While it's important to evoke emotions, it's equally important to balance them. Avoid overwhelming the audience with too much emotion, which can lead to desensitization or disengagement.
4. **Use a Consistent Tone:** Maintain a consistent emotional tone throughout your copy. This helps reinforce the emotional connection and prevents confusion.
5. **Test and Optimize:** Continuously test different approaches to see which ones resonate most with your audience. Use feedback and data to refine your emotional appeals.

Conclusion

Emotional resonance is a powerful tool in copywriting. By understanding and strategically evoking emotions, you can create content that captures attention, creates memorable impressions, and drives action. In the next chapter, we will explore how to tap into cognitive biases to craft compelling copy.

Chapter 6: How to Tap into Cognitive Biases to Craft Compelling Copy

Understanding Cognitive Biases

Cognitive biases are systematic patterns of deviation from rationality in judgment, which can influence decision-making processes. These biases affect how people perceive information and make decisions, often leading them to choose options that seem irrational from a purely logical perspective. By understanding these biases, copywriters can craft messages that align with these natural thought processes, making their copy more persuasive and effective.

Key Cognitive Biases in Copywriting

1. **Anchoring Bias:** People rely heavily on the first piece of information they encounter (the "anchor") when making decisions. Presenting a high initial price before offering a discount can make the discounted price seem more attractive.

2. **Confirmation Bias:** Individuals favor information that confirms their preexisting beliefs or values. Crafting messages that align with the audience's beliefs can enhance receptiveness.

3. **Bandwagon Effect:** People tend to adopt behaviors or beliefs because many others are doing the same. Highlighting the popularity of a product or service can

increase its attractiveness.

4. **Loss Aversion:** The fear of losing something is more powerful than the pleasure of gaining something of equal value. Emphasizing potential losses can be a strong motivator for action.

5. **Recency Effect:** People tend to remember the most recent information better. Placing the most important information or call to action at the end of your message can make it more memorable.

6. **Framing Effect:** The way information is presented can significantly affect decisions. Positive framing (emphasizing benefits) and negative framing (emphasizing costs or losses) can influence perceptions and actions.

Techniques for Leveraging Cognitive Biases

1. **Anchoring:** Use a high initial price point to make subsequent offers seem more appealing. For example, "Originally $199, now only $99!"

2. **Confirmation Bias:** Craft messages that resonate with the audience's existing beliefs. For example, if your audience values sustainability, emphasize your product's eco-friendly aspects.

3. **Bandwagon Effect:** Highlight the popularity of your product or service. For example, "Join thousands of satisfied customers who have already made the switch."

4. **Loss Aversion:** Focus on what the audience stands to lose if they don't act. For example, "Don't miss out on this limited-time offer—save $50 today."

5. **Recency Effect:** Place the most crucial information or call to action at the end of your message. For example, "Act now to secure your spot before it's too late."

6. **Framing Effect:** Present information in a way that

aligns with your desired outcome. For example, "Enjoy a 20% discount" (positive framing) vs. "Don't miss out on saving 20%" (negative framing).

Practical Examples of Cognitive Biases in Copywriting

- **Anchoring Bias:** "Compare our premium plan at $199 to our standard plan at just $99. You're getting a great deal!"
- **Confirmation Bias:** "As a community dedicated to healthy living, we know you'll appreciate our organic, all-natural products."
- **Bandwagon Effect:** "Join the millions who have already discovered the benefits of our service."
- **Loss Aversion:** "Avoid the regret of missing this exclusive deal—act now!"
- **Recency Effect:** "Sign up today to get started. Remember, the offer ends soon!"
- **Framing Effect:** "Gain peace of mind with our 24/7 customer support" vs. "Don't be left in the dark without our 24/7 customer support."

Ethical Considerations

While cognitive biases can be powerful tools in copywriting, it's important to use them ethically. Manipulative tactics or deceit can damage your reputation and erode trust with your audience. Always aim to provide genuine value and ensure that your messages are honest and transparent.

Conclusion

Tapping into cognitive biases allows copywriters to craft messages that align with natural human thought processes, making their copy more persuasive and effective. By understanding and leveraging these biases, you can create compelling copy that resonates with your audience and drives action. In the next chapter, we will explore the various psychological techniques you can employ to enhance your

copywriting further.

Chapter 7: Psychological Techniques to Enhance Your Copy

Introduction to Psychological Techniques

Psychological techniques in copywriting leverage human behavior and cognitive processes to create persuasive and engaging messages. These techniques can enhance the effectiveness of your copy by tapping into the mental and emotional triggers that drive decision-making. In this chapter, we'll explore various psychological techniques you can use to make your copy more compelling.

Key Psychological Techniques

1. **Priming:** Priming involves subtly influencing the audience's response by exposing them to specific stimuli beforehand. For example, using positive words at the beginning of your copy can create a favorable mindset, making the rest of the message more persuasive.
2. **Repetition:** Repetition increases familiarity and trust. Repeating key messages or phrases throughout your copy can reinforce your main points and make them more memorable.
3. **Contrast:** Contrast highlights the differences between options, making one option appear more attractive. For example, presenting a high-priced product alongside

a lower-priced one can make the lower-priced option seem like a better deal.

4. **Reciprocity:** As mentioned earlier, offering something of value first can create a sense of obligation. This technique can be used to build goodwill and increase the likelihood of a positive response.

5. **Scarcity and Urgency:** Emphasizing limited availability or time-sensitive offers can create a sense of urgency, prompting immediate action.

6. **Social Proof:** Leveraging testimonials, reviews, and endorsements from others can build credibility and trust, encouraging the audience to follow suit.

7. **Commitment and Consistency:** Encouraging small initial commitments can lead to larger actions. People like to be consistent with their previous actions and commitments.

8. **Storytelling:** Stories engage the audience on an emotional level, making the message more relatable and memorable. A well-crafted story can incorporate multiple psychological techniques.

9. **Authority:** Featuring endorsements from experts or authoritative figures can enhance credibility and trust, making your message more persuasive.

10. **Anchoring:** Setting a high reference point can make subsequent offers seem more attractive. For example, presenting a high original price before offering a discount.

Practical Applications of Psychological Techniques

1. **Priming:** Start your copy with positive words or concepts to set a favorable tone. For example, "Imagine experiencing the joy of effortless cooking with our innovative kitchen gadgets."

2. **Repetition:** Repeat key messages or phrases to

reinforce your main points. For example, "Our product is reliable, affordable, and effective."

3. **Contrast:** Present high-priced and lower-priced options side by side to highlight the value of the lower-priced option. For example, "Our premium plan is $199, but you can get all essential features in our standard plan for just $99."

4. **Reciprocity:** Offer free resources or valuable content to build goodwill. For example, "Download our free eBook to learn top strategies for success."

5. **Scarcity and Urgency:** Use phrases like "Limited time offer" or "Only a few left" to create urgency. For example, "Act now—offer ends soon!"

6. **Social Proof:** Include testimonials and user reviews to build credibility. For example, "Join thousands of satisfied customers who have transformed their lives with our product."

7. **Commitment and Consistency:** Start with small asks, like signing up for a newsletter, before moving to larger requests. For example, "Sign up for our free trial today—no credit card required."

8. **Storytelling:** Craft a relatable story that incorporates emotional elements. For example, "Meet Jane, a busy mom who struggled to find time for herself until she discovered our time-saving solutions."

9. **Authority:** Feature endorsements from experts or industry leaders. For example, "As recommended by leading nutritionists, our product is the best choice for a healthy lifestyle."

10. **Anchoring:** Present a high original price before offering a discount. For example, "Originally $299, now only $149!"

Ethical Considerations

When using psychological techniques, it's essential to do so ethically. Manipulative or deceitful tactics can harm your reputation and erode trust with your audience. Always aim to provide genuine value, be honest, and ensure that your messages align with your brand values.

Conclusion

Psychological techniques can significantly enhance the effectiveness of your copy by tapping into the mental and emotional triggers that drive decision-making. By understanding and applying these techniques, you can create more persuasive and engaging messages. In the next chapter, we will delve into the importance of understanding your audience and tailoring your copy to meet their specific needs and preferences.

Chapter 8: Understanding Your Audience

The Importance of Knowing Your Audience

Understanding your audience is crucial for creating effective and persuasive copy. Knowing who they are, what they need, and what motivates them allows you to tailor your messages to resonate deeply and drive the desired actions. Audience insights help you address their pain points, fulfill their desires, and speak their language, making your copy more relevant and compelling.

Key Aspects of Understanding Your Audience

1. **Demographics:** Age, gender, income, education level, and occupation provide a basic understanding of who your audience is. These factors can influence preferences and behaviors.
2. **Psychographics:** These include attitudes, values, interests, and lifestyles. Understanding psychographics helps you connect on a deeper emotional level.
3. **Pain Points:** Identifying the problems or challenges your audience faces allows you to offer solutions that address their specific needs.
4. **Desires and Goals:** Knowing what your audience wants to achieve enables you to position your product or service to fulfill those desires.
5. **Buying Behavior:** Understanding how your audience

makes purchasing decisions, including their preferred channels and influences, helps you craft messages that align with their buying journey.

6. **Language and Tone:** Adopting the language, tone, and style that resonates with your audience makes your copy more relatable and engaging.

Techniques for Understanding Your Audience

1. **Surveys and Questionnaires:** Conducting surveys allows you to gather direct feedback from your audience about their preferences, needs, and behaviors.
2. **Interviews:** In-depth interviews provide qualitative insights into your audience's motivations, challenges, and decision-making processes.
3. **Analytics:** Analyzing website, social media, and email analytics can reveal patterns in audience behavior and preferences.
4. **Social Listening:** Monitoring social media conversations about your brand, industry, or competitors helps you understand what your audience is talking about and how they feel.
5. **Customer Feedback:** Regularly collecting and analyzing feedback from your customers provides valuable insights into their experiences and needs.
6. **Competitor Analysis:** Studying your competitors' audience can provide insights into the market and identify opportunities to better meet your audience's needs.

Creating Audience Personas

Audience personas are fictional, generalized representations of your ideal customers. They help you visualize and understand your audience better, guiding your copywriting efforts to be more targeted and effective.

Steps to Create Audience Personas:
1. **Research:** Gather data from various sources like surveys, interviews, and analytics.
2. **Identify Patterns:** Look for common traits, behaviors, and preferences in the data.
3. **Create Profiles:** Develop detailed profiles for each persona, including demographics, psychographics, pain points, goals, and buying behavior.
4. **Use Personas:** Reference these personas when creating copy to ensure your messages are tailored to the specific needs and preferences of your audience.

Practical Tips for Tailoring Your Copy
1. **Address Pain Points:** Highlight how your product or service solves specific problems your audience faces.
2. **Use Relatable Language:** Adopt the language and tone that resonates with your audience. Avoid jargon unless it's commonly used by your audience.
3. **Focus on Benefits:** Emphasize the benefits and outcomes that matter most to your audience, rather than just listing features.
4. **Incorporate Social Proof:** Use testimonials, reviews, and case studies from people who resemble your audience to build trust and credibility.
5. **Create a Sense of Belonging:** Show that you understand your audience's values and aspirations, making them feel part of a community.
6. **Test and Iterate:** Continuously test different approaches and gather feedback to refine your messages and ensure they resonate with your audience.

Conclusion

Understanding your audience is the foundation of effective

copywriting. By gaining deep insights into who they are, what they need, and what motivates them, you can create tailored messages that resonate deeply and drive action. In the next chapter, we will explore the importance of crafting a strong value proposition and how to communicate it effectively.

Chapter 9: Crafting a Strong Value Proposition

What is a Value Proposition?

A value proposition is a clear, concise statement that articulates the unique benefits and value your product or service provides to your target audience. It explains why your offering is better than competitors' and why customers should choose you. A strong value proposition is crucial for capturing attention, generating interest, and driving conversions.

Elements of a Strong Value Proposition

1. **Clarity:** Your value proposition should be easy to understand. Avoid jargon and complex language.
2. **Specificity:** Highlight specific benefits and features that set your product or service apart.
3. **Relevance:** Address the specific needs and pain points of your target audience.
4. **Uniqueness:** Differentiate your offering from competitors by emphasizing what makes it unique.
5. **Promise of Value:** Clearly state the value or outcome the customer can expect from your product or service.

Crafting Your Value Proposition

1. **Identify Your Target Audience:** Understand who your ideal customers are and what they need.

2. **Define the Problem:** Clearly articulate the problem or pain point your product or service addresses.
3. **Highlight Key Benefits:** Focus on the most compelling benefits that your product or service provides.
4. **Differentiate Your Offering:** Identify what makes your product or service unique and better than competitors.
5. **Summarize in a Clear Statement:** Combine these elements into a concise statement that communicates your value proposition.

Examples of Strong Value Propositions

- **Slack:** "Slack brings all your communication together in one place. It's real-time messaging, archiving, and search for modern teams."
- **Dollar Shave Club:** "A great shave for a few bucks a month. No commitment, no fees, no BS."
- **Evernote:** "Remember everything. Capture, organize, and share notes from anywhere. Your best ideas are always with you and always in sync."

Testing and Refining Your Value Proposition

1. **A/B Testing:** Test different versions of your value proposition to see which one resonates best with your audience.
2. **Customer Feedback:** Gather feedback from your customers to understand how they perceive your value proposition.
3. **Analyze Competitors:** Study your competitors' value propositions to identify gaps and opportunities for differentiation.
4. **Iterate and Improve:** Continuously refine your value proposition based on feedback and testing results.

Communicating Your Value Proposition

1. **Homepage:** Your value proposition should be

prominently displayed on your homepage, as it's often the first thing visitors see.

2. **Landing Pages:** Use targeted value propositions on landing pages to address specific audience segments and their needs.
3. **Marketing Materials:** Ensure your value proposition is consistent across all marketing materials, including emails, ads, and social media.
4. **Sales Conversations:** Train your sales team to effectively communicate your value proposition during sales calls and meetings.

Practical Tips for Crafting a Value Proposition

1. **Be Clear and Concise:** Avoid vague language and long-winded explanations. Get to the point quickly.
2. **Focus on Benefits:** Emphasize the benefits your product or service provides rather than just listing features.
3. **Use Customer Language:** Speak in the language of your customers, using words and phrases they relate to.
4. **Highlight Outcomes:** Clearly state the positive outcomes or results customers can expect from using your product or service.
5. **Test for Effectiveness:** Continuously test and refine your value proposition to ensure it resonates with your audience and drives conversions.

Conclusion

A strong value proposition is essential for capturing the attention of your target audience and persuading them to choose your product or service over competitors. By clearly articulating the unique benefits and value you provide, you can create a compelling message that drives interest and action. In the next chapter, we will explore the role of storytelling in copywriting and how to craft engaging stories that resonate with your audience.

Chapter 10: The Role of Storytelling in Copywriting

Why Storytelling Matters

Storytelling is a powerful tool in copywriting because it engages the audience emotionally and makes your message more relatable and memorable. Stories can simplify complex information, illustrate key points, and create a deeper connection with your audience. When done effectively, storytelling can enhance your copy by making it more engaging and persuasive.

Elements of a Compelling Story

1. **Character:** The character is the central figure in your story. This could be a customer, an employee, or even your brand. The character should be relatable and evoke empathy from your audience.

2. **Conflict:** The conflict is the challenge or problem the character faces. This element is crucial because it creates tension and keeps the audience engaged. The conflict should align with the pain points or challenges your audience experiences.

3. **Resolution:** The resolution is how the character overcomes the conflict. This is where you demonstrate the value of your product or service. The resolution should provide a clear and compelling solution to the

problem.

4. **Emotion:** Emotions are the driving force behind effective storytelling. Your story should evoke emotions that resonate with your audience, such as joy, fear, empathy, or inspiration.

Types of Stories in Copywriting

1. **Customer Success Stories:** These stories showcase how your product or service helped a customer overcome a challenge and achieve their goals. They serve as powerful testimonials and social proof.
2. **Brand Stories:** These stories share the journey, values, and mission of your brand. They help humanize your brand and build a deeper connection with your audience.
3. **Product Stories:** These stories focus on how your product or service was developed, highlighting its unique features and benefits. They can help differentiate your product from competitors.
4. **Educational Stories:** These stories provide valuable information or insights to your audience in an engaging way. They position your brand as a thought leader and build trust with your audience.

Techniques for Effective Storytelling

1. **Use a Clear Structure:** Follow a clear structure with a beginning, middle, and end. Introduce the character and conflict, build tension, and provide a satisfying resolution.
2. **Make it Relatable:** Ensure your story is relevant and relatable to your audience. Use characters, settings, and scenarios that reflect their experiences and challenges.
3. **Incorporate Details:** Include specific details that make your story vivid and believable. Use descriptive

language to paint a picture and immerse the audience in the story.

4. **Show, Don't Tell:** Instead of just telling your audience about the benefits of your product, show them through the story. Demonstrate how your product made a difference in the character's life.

5. **Use Dialogue:** Incorporate dialogue to make your story more dynamic and engaging. Dialogue can reveal character personalities and make the story more relatable.

6. **Evoke Emotions:** Focus on evoking the right emotions in your audience. Use emotional triggers that resonate with their values and desires.

Practical Examples of Storytelling in Copywriting

- **Customer Success Story:** "Jane was a busy working mom who struggled to find time for herself. She discovered our fitness app and started with short, guided workouts. In just a few months, Jane felt more energized and confident. Now, she never misses a workout and has achieved her fitness goals."

- **Brand Story:** "Our journey began in a small garage, where two friends had a vision to create eco-friendly products. Today, we are proud to be a leading sustainable brand, committed to reducing our environmental footprint and making a positive impact on the planet."

- **Product Story:** "Our new noise-canceling headphones were developed after extensive research and testing. With advanced technology and ergonomic design, they provide an unparalleled listening experience, allowing you to enjoy your favorite music without any distractions."

- **Educational Story:** "Imagine waking up every morning feeling refreshed and ready to tackle the day. Our sleep experts have developed a guide to help you improve your sleep quality, with tips on creating a relaxing bedtime routine and optimizing your sleep environment."

Conclusion

Storytelling is a powerful technique in copywriting that can make your message more engaging, relatable, and memorable. By crafting compelling stories that resonate with your audience, you can enhance the effectiveness of your copy and drive action. In the next chapter, we will explore the psychology behind creating urgency and scarcity in your copy to prompt immediate action from your audience.

Chapter 11: Creating Urgency and Scarcity in Your Copy

The Psychology Behind Urgency and Scarcity

Urgency and scarcity are powerful psychological triggers that can prompt immediate action from your audience. These principles are based on the fear of missing out (FOMO) and the desire to avoid loss. When people perceive that a product or offer is limited or time-sensitive, they are more likely to act quickly to secure it.

The Benefits of Urgency and Scarcity

1. **Increased Conversions:** Urgency and scarcity can lead to higher conversion rates by motivating customers to act quickly.
2. **Reduced Decision-Making Time:** These tactics can shorten the decision-making process, as customers are prompted to make quicker choices.
3. **Enhanced Perceived Value:** Limited availability can increase the perceived value of a product or offer, making it more desirable.

Techniques for Creating Urgency

1. **Limited-Time Offers:** Create promotions that are available for a short period. Use phrases like "Hurry, offer ends soon!" or "24-hour sale."
2. **Countdown Timers:** Use countdown timers on your

website or in your emails to visually represent the time remaining for an offer. This creates a sense of immediacy.

3. **Seasonal Promotions:** Tie your offers to holidays or special events to create a natural sense of urgency. For example, "Get 20% off during our Black Friday sale."

4. **Exclusive Deals:** Offer special deals that are only available to a select group, such as email subscribers or loyalty program members. For example, "Exclusive offer for our VIP members—act now!"

Techniques for Creating Scarcity

1. **Limited Stock:** Highlight the limited availability of a product. Use phrases like "Only 5 left in stock" or "While supplies last."

2. **Exclusive Products:** Offer products that are available for a limited time or in limited quantities. For example, "Limited edition items—get yours before they're gone!"

3. **Limited Access:** Provide access to services or memberships for a limited number of people. For example, "Join our beta program—only 50 spots available."

4. **Sold-Out Alerts:** Show that certain items are sold out to create a sense of urgency for other products. For example, "Hurry, this item is almost sold out!"

Practical Examples of Urgency and Scarcity in Copy

- **Limited-Time Offer:** "Don't miss out on our summer sale! Save 30% on all items—offer ends in 48 hours."
- **Countdown Timer:** "Flash sale! Only 3 hours left to get 50% off. [Insert countdown timer]"
- **Limited Stock:** "Hurry, only 3 units left in stock. Order now to secure your item."
- **Exclusive Deal:** "Special offer for our newsletter subscribers—get 20% off your next purchase. Act fast!"

- **Limited Edition:** "Introducing our limited-edition holiday collection. Available only while supplies last."

Ethical Considerations

While creating urgency and scarcity can be effective, it's important to use these tactics ethically. Avoid false claims or misleading statements about limited availability or time-sensitive offers. Being transparent and honest with your audience builds trust and credibility, which are essential for long-term success.

Best Practices for Implementing Urgency and Scarcity

1. **Be Honest:** Always be truthful about the availability and timing of your offers. Avoid creating false scarcity.
2. **Use Clear Language:** Clearly communicate the urgency or scarcity in your copy. Ensure your audience understands the limited nature of the offer.
3. **Provide Value:** Ensure that your limited-time or scarce offers provide genuine value to your audience. Don't use these tactics just to drive sales; make sure the offer is worth their attention.
4. **Test and Measure:** Continuously test different approaches to see what resonates best with your audience. Measure the impact on conversions and adjust your strategies accordingly.

Conclusion

Creating urgency and scarcity in your copy can effectively prompt immediate action from your audience by leveraging the fear of missing out and the desire to avoid loss. By using these techniques ethically and strategically, you can increase conversions, shorten decision-making times, and enhance the perceived value of your offers. In the next chapter, we will explore the impact of visual elements in copywriting and how to use them effectively to enhance your message.

Chapter 12: The Impact of Visual Elements in Copywriting

Why Visual Elements Matter

Visual elements play a crucial role in copywriting by enhancing the readability, engagement, and overall impact of your message. They help to break up large blocks of text, make the content more appealing, and can convey information more effectively than words alone. In this chapter, we'll explore various visual elements and how to use them effectively in your copy.

Types of Visual Elements

1. **Images:** Relevant and high-quality images can illustrate points, evoke emotions, and capture attention. They should complement and enhance your written content.
2. **Infographics:** Infographics present complex information in a visually appealing and easy-to-understand format. They are useful for summarizing data, explaining processes, and highlighting key points.
3. **Videos:** Videos can engage your audience more deeply than text or images alone. They are effective for demonstrating products, telling stories, and providing tutorials.

4. **Charts and Graphs:** Charts and graphs visually represent data, making it easier for your audience to grasp and remember key statistics and trends.

5. **Icons:** Icons can replace text to simplify information and make it more visually appealing. They are useful for indicating features, benefits, and actions.

6. **Typography:** The choice of fonts, sizes, and styles can influence readability and the overall tone of your copy. Good typography can highlight important information and create a visual hierarchy.

7. **Color:** Color can evoke emotions, draw attention, and enhance brand identity. It's important to use color strategically to support your message and create visual interest.

Best Practices for Using Visual Elements

1. **Choose Relevant Images:** Select images that are directly related to your content and reinforce your message. Avoid generic stock photos that don't add value.

2. **Maintain Quality:** Ensure all visual elements are high-quality and professional. Poor-quality visuals can detract from your message and reduce credibility.

3. **Use Infographics Wisely:** Create infographics to present data and complex information. Ensure they are well-designed and easy to read.

4. **Incorporate Videos:** Use videos to engage your audience but keep them concise and focused. Ensure they are professionally produced and relevant to your message.

5. **Simplify with Icons:** Use icons to break up text and make your content more digestible. Ensure they are clear and easily understood.

6. **Optimize Typography:** Choose fonts that are easy to

read and match the tone of your copy. Use different font sizes and styles to create a visual hierarchy and highlight important information.

7. **Strategic Use of Color:** Use color to draw attention to key elements, evoke emotions, and reinforce your brand identity. Ensure there is enough contrast for readability.

Practical Examples of Visual Elements in Copywriting

- **Images:** Use before-and-after images to show the effectiveness of a product. For example, a skincare brand can show the transformation in skin quality after using their product.
- **Infographics:** Create an infographic to explain a complicated process, such as the steps involved in applying for a loan.
- **Videos:** Include a video tutorial demonstrating how to use a new software feature.
- **Charts and Graphs:** Use a bar chart to compare the performance of your product against competitors.
- **Icons:** Use checkmark icons to list the features and benefits of a service.
- **Typography:** Use a larger, bold font for headlines and smaller, regular font for body text. Highlight important points with different colors or italicization.
- **Color:** Use your brand colors to create a cohesive look. Use contrasting colors to draw attention to call-to-action buttons.

Tools for Creating Visual Elements

1. **Canva:** A user-friendly design tool for creating images, infographics, and other visuals.
2. **Adobe Spark:** An easy-to-use tool for creating graphics, videos, and web pages.
3. **Piktochart:** A tool specifically for creating infographics

and presentations.

4. **Lumen5:** A video creation tool that turns blog posts and articles into engaging videos.
5. **Visme:** A versatile tool for creating infographics, presentations, and other visual content.

Conclusion

Incorporating visual elements into your copy can significantly enhance its effectiveness by making it more engaging, readable, and memorable. By choosing relevant and high-quality visuals, you can support your message and create a more compelling experience for your audience. In the next chapter, we will discuss the importance of crafting effective calls to action (CTAs) and how to optimize them for maximum impact.

Chapter 13: Crafting Effective Calls to Action (CTAs)

What is a Call to Action (CTA)?

A call to action (CTA) is a prompt that encourages your audience to take a specific action. CTAs are essential in guiding your audience towards the desired outcome, whether it's making a purchase, signing up for a newsletter, downloading a resource, or any other goal. Effective CTAs are clear, compelling, and actionable.

The Importance of CTAs

1. **Driving Conversions:** CTAs are critical for converting visitors into leads, customers, or subscribers. They guide users towards the next step in their journey.
2. **Providing Direction:** Clear CTAs eliminate confusion and provide a clear path for users to follow, enhancing the overall user experience.
3. **Encouraging Engagement:** Well-crafted CTAs can increase user engagement by prompting them to interact with your content, share information, or participate in offers.

Key Elements of an Effective CTA

1. **Clarity:** Your CTA should be clear and easy to understand. Avoid ambiguous language and ensure the action you want the user to take is obvious.

2. **Actionable Language:** Use strong, action-oriented verbs that clearly communicate what the user should do. Examples include "Buy Now," "Sign Up," "Download," and "Learn More."
3. **Value Proposition:** Highlight the benefit or value the user will receive by taking the action. For example, "Get Your Free Ebook" or "Save 20% Today."
4. **Urgency:** Creating a sense of urgency can prompt immediate action. Phrases like "Limited Time Offer" or "Act Now" can be effective.
5. **Visibility:** Ensure your CTA stands out visually. Use contrasting colors, larger fonts, and strategic placement to draw attention.
6. **Relevance:** Tailor your CTA to the specific context and audience. A relevant CTA is more likely to resonate and prompt action.

Crafting CTAs for Different Goals

1. **Sales:** Use CTAs like "Shop Now," "Add to Cart," or "Buy Today" to drive purchases.
2. **Lead Generation:** Use CTAs such as "Download Your Free Guide," "Get a Free Quote," or "Join Our Newsletter" to capture leads.
3. **Content Engagement:** Use CTAs like "Read More," "Watch Video," or "Share This Post" to encourage interaction with your content.
4. **Event Registrations:** Use CTAs such as "Register Now," "Reserve Your Spot," or "Sign Up Today" to increase event participation.
5. **Service Inquiries:** Use CTAs like "Request a Consultation," "Get in Touch," or "Contact Us" to encourage inquiries about your services.

Examples of Effective CTAs

- **Ecommerce:** "Shop the Sale – Up to 50% Off!"

- **Lead Magnet:** "Download Your Free Ebook Now"
- **Newsletter Signup:** "Join Our Community – Subscribe Today"
- **Event Registration:** "Save Your Seat – Register for the Webinar"
- **Service Inquiry:** "Schedule Your Free Consultation"

A/B Testing Your CTAs

1. **Test Different Wording:** Experiment with different phrasing to see which version resonates best with your audience.
2. **Test Different Designs:** Try various colors, sizes, and placements to determine the most effective design for your CTA.
3. **Test Different Offers:** If applicable, test different value propositions to see which offer generates the most responses.
4. **Measure Results:** Use analytics to track the performance of your CTAs and identify the best-performing variations.

Best Practices for Implementing CTAs

1. **Use One Primary CTA:** Focus on one main CTA per page or section to avoid overwhelming the user with too many choices.
2. **Make it Prominent:** Ensure your CTA stands out visually and is easy to find. Use contrasting colors and strategic placement.
3. **Keep it Simple:** Use concise and straightforward language to avoid confusion and ensure clarity.
4. **Align with User Intent:** Ensure your CTA aligns with the user's current stage in their journey and the content they are engaging with.
5. **Create a Sense of Urgency:** Encourage immediate

action by highlighting limited time offers or exclusive deals.

Conclusion

Crafting effective calls to action is essential for guiding your audience towards the desired actions and driving conversions. By using clear, actionable language, highlighting the value proposition, and creating a sense of urgency, you can create compelling CTAs that prompt immediate responses. In the next chapter, we will explore the role of social proof in copywriting and how to leverage it to build trust and credibility.

Chapter 14: Leveraging Social Proof in Copywriting

What is Social Proof?

Social proof is a psychological phenomenon where people look to the actions and opinions of others to determine their own. In the context of marketing and copywriting, social proof can take various forms such as testimonials, reviews, case studies, endorsements, and user-generated content. It is a powerful tool for building trust and credibility, influencing potential customers' decisions.

The Importance of Social Proof

1. **Builds Trust:** Social proof reassures potential customers that others have had positive experiences with your product or service.
2. **Reduces Uncertainty:** It helps alleviate doubts and concerns by showing that others have successfully used and benefited from your offering.
3. **Enhances Credibility:** Featuring endorsements from reputable sources or satisfied customers can enhance your brand's credibility.
4. **Increases Conversions:** By showcasing positive experiences and outcomes, social proof can influence purchasing decisions and boost conversions.

Types of Social Proof

1. **Customer Testimonials:** Written or video testimonials from satisfied customers sharing their positive experiences with your product or service.
2. **Reviews and Ratings:** User reviews and ratings on platforms like Google, Yelp, Amazon, or your website.
3. **Case Studies:** Detailed accounts of how your product or service helped a specific customer solve a problem or achieve a goal.
4. **Endorsements:** Recommendations from industry experts, influencers, or celebrities who support your product or service.
5. **User-Generated Content:** Content created by your customers, such as photos, videos, or social media posts showcasing your product in use.
6. **Social Media Proof:** Likes, shares, comments, and mentions on social media platforms.
7. **Trust Badges and Certifications:** Logos of awards, certifications, partnerships, or memberships in reputable organizations.

How to Incorporate Social Proof in Your Copy

1. **Highlight Testimonials:** Feature customer testimonials prominently on your website, landing pages, and marketing materials. Use real names and photos to enhance credibility.
2. **Showcase Reviews and Ratings:** Display user reviews and ratings on product pages, emphasizing high ratings and positive feedback.
3. **Share Case Studies:** Create detailed case studies that demonstrate the specific benefits and outcomes your product or service provided. Include data and quotes from the customer.
4. **Feature Endorsements:** Highlight endorsements from industry experts, influencers, or celebrities. Use their

quotes and images to add authority to your claims.

5. **Leverage User-Generated Content:** Share user-generated content on your website and social media channels. Encourage customers to share their experiences and tag your brand.

6. **Display Social Media Proof:** Show the number of likes, shares, and comments your posts receive. Highlight positive mentions and interactions.

7. **Use Trust Badges and Certifications:** Display logos of awards, certifications, and reputable partnerships to build trust and credibility.

Practical Examples of Social Proof

- **Testimonial:** "I've been using this product for a year, and it has significantly improved my daily routine. Highly recommended!" – Jane D.
- **Review and Rating:** "4.8/5 stars based on 1,200 reviews."
- **Case Study:** "Discover how Company X increased their sales by 30% using our software. Read the full case study."
- **Endorsement:** "As an industry expert, I trust and recommend this product for its reliability and performance." – John Smith, Tech Influencer
- **User-Generated Content:** "Check out how our customers are using our product! Share your own photos with #OurProduct."
- **Social Media Proof:** "Join our community of 50,000+ happy customers on Instagram!"
- **Trust Badge:** "Certified by the Better Business Bureau – A+ Rating"

Best Practices for Using Social Proof

1. **Be Authentic:** Use genuine testimonials and reviews. Authenticity is key to building trust with your

audience.

2. **Be Specific:** Include specific details and results in your social proof to make it more compelling and credible.
3. **Update Regularly:** Keep your social proof up to date to reflect the latest customer experiences and endorsements.
4. **Show Diversity:** Feature a diverse range of customers to appeal to different segments of your audience.
5. **Use Visuals:** Incorporate images and videos to make your social proof more engaging and impactful.
6. **Ask for Permission:** Always obtain permission from customers before using their testimonials, reviews, or user-generated content.

Conclusion

Leveraging social proof in your copywriting is an effective way to build trust, reduce uncertainty, and enhance credibility. By showcasing positive experiences and endorsements from others, you can influence potential customers' decisions and increase conversions. In the next chapter, we will discuss the importance of understanding your audience and how to tailor your copy to their needs and preferences.

Chapter 15: The Importance of Consistency in Copywriting

Why Consistency Matters

Consistency in copywriting is crucial for building a strong and recognizable brand. When your messaging is consistent across all channels, it reinforces your brand identity, builds trust with your audience, and ensures that your communication is clear and effective. Consistency helps your audience to recognize and remember your brand, fostering loyalty and engagement.

Elements of Consistency in Copywriting

1. **Brand Voice:** Your brand voice is the distinct personality and style of your brand's communication. It should be consistent across all your copy to create a cohesive and recognizable brand image.
2. **Tone:** The tone of your copy can vary depending on the context but should still align with your overall brand voice. Whether formal, casual, humorous, or serious, the tone should be appropriate for the audience and the message.
3. **Messaging:** The core messages and key selling points of your brand should remain consistent. This includes your value propositions, mission statements, and taglines.

4. **Visual Style:** While not strictly part of copywriting, the visual elements such as fonts, colors, and layout should also be consistent and complement the written content.
5. **Terminology and Phrasing:** Use the same terminology, phrasing, and style across all your content to avoid confusion and reinforce familiarity.

Benefits of Consistency

1. **Builds Brand Recognition:** Consistent messaging helps your audience easily recognize your brand across different platforms and touchpoints.
2. **Enhances Trust:** Consistency in your communication builds trust and credibility. Your audience knows what to expect from your brand.
3. **Improves Clarity:** Clear and consistent messaging ensures that your audience understands your brand's value and offerings without confusion.
4. **Strengthens Brand Identity:** A cohesive and consistent brand voice strengthens your overall brand identity, making it more memorable and impactful.
5. **Increases Engagement:** When your audience feels a sense of familiarity and reliability with your brand, they are more likely to engage with your content and become loyal customers.

How to Maintain Consistency

1. **Develop a Style Guide:** Create a comprehensive style guide that outlines your brand voice, tone, messaging, terminology, and visual style. Ensure all team members and contributors adhere to these guidelines.
2. **Train Your Team:** Provide training and resources for your team to understand and implement the style guide. Regularly update them on any changes or new guidelines.

3. **Use Templates:** Create templates for common types of content, such as emails, social media posts, and blog articles. This ensures a consistent format and style.
4. **Review and Edit:** Implement a review process to ensure all content aligns with your style guide before it is published. Regularly audit your content to maintain consistency.
5. **Centralize Content Creation:** Whenever possible, centralize content creation to a dedicated team or individual who is well-versed in your brand's style and guidelines.

Practical Examples of Consistent Copywriting

- **Emails:** Use a consistent greeting, sign-off, and format for all your emails. Ensure the language and tone match your brand voice.
- **Social Media:** Use the same profile picture, bio, and hashtags across all social media platforms. Maintain a consistent posting style and frequency.
- **Website:** Ensure your website content, from the homepage to product descriptions, follows a unified style and messaging. Use the same fonts, colors, and layout throughout.
- **Advertising:** Your advertisements should reflect the same brand voice and tone as your other content. Ensure your key messages and visual elements are consistent.
- **Customer Support:** Train your customer support team to use the same language and tone as your marketing content. Provide them with scripts and templates that align with your brand voice.

Tools for Ensuring Consistency

1. **Style Guide Tools:** Tools like Canva's Brand Kit or Frontify help you create and manage your brand style

guide.

2. **Content Management Systems (CMS):** A CMS like WordPress or HubSpot allows you to maintain consistency in your website content.
3. **Social Media Management Tools:** Tools like Hootsuite or Buffer help you schedule and manage social media posts, ensuring consistency in your messaging and timing.
4. **Email Marketing Platforms:** Platforms like Mailchimp or Constant Contact allow you to create templates and automate emails, maintaining consistency in your email marketing.
5. **Collaboration Tools:** Tools like Slack or Trello facilitate team communication and collaboration, ensuring everyone is on the same page with your brand guidelines.

Conclusion

Consistency in copywriting is essential for building a strong, recognizable, and trustworthy brand. By maintaining a consistent brand voice, tone, messaging, and visual style, you can enhance brand recognition, build trust, and improve engagement with your audience. In the next chapter, we will explore the role of storytelling in copywriting and how to use it to connect with your audience on a deeper level.

Chapter 16: Using Humor in Copywriting

Why Use Humor in Copywriting?

Humor can be a highly effective tool in copywriting when used appropriately. It can make your content more engaging, memorable, and shareable. Humor helps to humanize your brand, making it more relatable and approachable. It can also break down barriers and make your audience more receptive to your message.

Benefits of Using Humor

1. **Engages the Audience:** Humor captures attention and keeps your audience engaged with your content.
2. **Makes Your Brand Memorable:** Funny content is often more memorable and can leave a lasting impression on your audience.
3. **Enhances Shareability:** Humorous content is more likely to be shared on social media, increasing your reach and visibility.
4. **Builds Rapport:** Humor can create a sense of camaraderie and connection with your audience, fostering loyalty and trust.
5. **Differentiates Your Brand:** A unique and humorous approach can set your brand apart from competitors and make it stand out in a crowded market.

Types of Humor in Copywriting

1. **Puns and Wordplay:** Clever use of language, puns, and wordplay can add a lighthearted touch to your copy.
2. **Anecdotes:** Sharing funny stories or personal experiences can make your copy more relatable and engaging.
3. **Sarcasm and Irony:** When used carefully, sarcasm and irony can add a witty edge to your content. However, it's important to ensure it aligns with your brand voice and audience.
4. **Visual Humor:** Incorporating funny images, memes, or cartoons can enhance the humor in your copy.
5. **Exaggeration:** Hyperbole and exaggerated statements can create a humorous effect and highlight the benefits of your product or service in a playful way.

How to Incorporate Humor Effectively

1. **Know Your Audience:** Understand your audience's sense of humor and what they find funny. Ensure your humor is appropriate and resonates with them.
2. **Align with Brand Voice:** Ensure that the humor aligns with your brand voice and personality. It should feel natural and consistent with your overall messaging.
3. **Be Respectful:** Avoid humor that could be offensive or alienating. Be mindful of cultural differences and sensitivities.
4. **Keep it Relevant:** Ensure the humor is relevant to your message and adds value to your content. Avoid using humor just for the sake of it.
5. **Test and Iterate:** Test different types of humor with your audience to see what resonates best. Use feedback to refine your approach.

Practical Examples of Humor in Copywriting

- **Product Descriptions:** "Our socks are so comfortable; you'll forget you're wearing them. Just don't forget to take them off before showering!"
- **Social Media Posts:** "Feeling down? Just remember, every time you buy our product, a unicorn gets its wings. Okay, maybe not, but it's still magical."
- **Email Campaigns:** "We noticed you left some items in your cart. Was it something we said? Let's make up – here's 10% off your order!"
- **Advertising:** "Our competitor's product claims to work miracles. We can't promise that, but we can promise you'll look fabulous using ours."

Best Practices for Using Humor

1. **Start Small:** Introduce humor gradually and see how your audience responds. Start with light-hearted language and puns before trying more bold humor.
2. **Use Visuals:** Pair your humorous copy with funny visuals to enhance the effect and create a more engaging experience.
3. **Stay True to Your Brand:** Ensure your humor is in line with your brand's values and mission. It should enhance your brand identity, not detract from it.
4. **Be Authentic:** Authentic humor is more likely to resonate with your audience. Avoid forcing jokes or trying too hard to be funny.
5. **Maintain Balance:** Use humor to complement your message, not overshadow it. Ensure the core message and value proposition remain clear.

Tools for Incorporating Humor

1. **Meme Generators:** Tools like Imgflip and Canva can help you create humorous memes and visuals.
2. **GIF Libraries:** Websites like Giphy and Tenor provide a vast library of GIFs to add humor to your content.

3. **Humor Writing Resources:** Books and online courses on humor writing can provide inspiration and techniques for incorporating humor into your copy.
4. **Social Media:** Platforms like Twitter and Instagram are great for experimenting with short, humorous content and engaging with your audience in a playful way.

Conclusion

Using humor in copywriting can make your content more engaging, memorable, and shareable. By understanding your audience, aligning with your brand voice, and using humor thoughtfully and respectfully, you can create content that resonates and stands out. In the next chapter, we will explore the principles of ethical copywriting and how to maintain integrity and trust in your messaging.

Chapter 17: Ethical Copywriting

Why Ethical Copywriting Matters

Ethical copywriting is crucial for building and maintaining trust with your audience. In an era where consumers are more informed and skeptical, transparency, honesty, and integrity are essential. Ethical copywriting ensures that your messaging is not only persuasive but also responsible and respectful.

Principles of Ethical Copywriting

1. **Honesty:** Always be truthful about your product or service. Avoid making exaggerated or false claims that could mislead your audience.
2. **Transparency:** Be clear and open about your intentions, whether you're selling a product, collecting data, or promoting a service. Transparency builds trust and credibility.
3. **Respect:** Show respect for your audience's time, intelligence, and privacy. Avoid manipulative tactics and respect their right to make informed decisions.
4. **Accuracy:** Ensure that all information provided is accurate and up to date. Misinformation can damage your credibility and lead to a loss of trust.
5. **Fairness:** Represent your competitors fairly and avoid disparaging remarks. Focus on highlighting your strengths without misleading comparisons.

Benefits of Ethical Copywriting
1. **Builds Trust:** Ethical copywriting fosters trust and credibility with your audience. Trust is essential for building long-term relationships and customer loyalty.
2. **Enhances Reputation:** A reputation for honesty and integrity can set your brand apart and attract more customers.
3. **Reduces Legal Risks:** Ethical practices reduce the risk of legal issues related to false advertising, misrepresentation, or privacy violations.
4. **Promotes Positive Brand Image:** Ethical copywriting contributes to a positive brand image and can enhance your brand's overall reputation and value.
5. **Encourages Customer Loyalty:** Customers are more likely to remain loyal to brands that they perceive as honest and trustworthy.

How to Practice Ethical Copywriting
1. **Avoid Exaggeration:** Be realistic and truthful about the benefits and capabilities of your product or service. Avoid using hyperbole or making promises you can't keep.
2. **Disclose Important Information:** Provide all necessary information for your audience to make an informed decision. This includes pricing, terms and conditions, and potential risks or side effects.
3. **Respect Privacy:** Be transparent about how you collect, use, and protect customer data. Ensure that your privacy policies are clear and accessible.
4. **Provide Accurate Comparisons:** If you compare your product to competitors, ensure that the comparisons are fair, accurate, and relevant.
5. **Use Clear Language:** Avoid using jargon or complex language that could confuse your audience. Clear

and simple language promotes understanding and transparency.

Practical Examples of Ethical Copywriting

- **Product Descriptions:** "Our skincare product is designed to help reduce the appearance of fine lines. Results may vary, and it's always best to consult with a dermatologist."
- **Advertising:** "Our software can improve efficiency by up to 20%. This estimate is based on customer feedback and case studies."
- **Email Marketing:** "We value your privacy. You're receiving this email because you signed up for our newsletter. If you no longer wish to receive updates, you can unsubscribe here."
- **Social Media:** "We're proud of our product's sustainability efforts. Learn more about our practices and the impact they have on the environment."

Best Practices for Ethical Copywriting

1. **Get Feedback:** Regularly seek feedback from your audience to ensure your messaging is clear, honest, and respectful.
2. **Stay Informed:** Keep up to date with industry standards and regulations related to advertising and marketing to ensure compliance.
3. **Create Guidelines:** Develop internal guidelines for ethical copywriting and ensure all team members are aware and adhere to them.
4. **Review Content:** Implement a review process to check for accuracy, honesty, and compliance with ethical standards before publishing any content.
5. **Promote Accountability:** Encourage a culture of accountability where team members feel responsible for maintaining ethical standards in all their work.

Tools for Ethical Copywriting

1. **Plagiarism Checkers:** Tools like Grammarly and Copyscape help ensure your content is original and not copied from other sources.
2. **Fact-Checking Tools:** Websites like Snopes and FactCheck.org can help verify the accuracy of claims and information.
3. **Privacy Compliance Tools:** Tools like OneTrust help manage and ensure compliance with privacy regulations like GDPR and CCPA.
4. **Editing and Review Tools:** Tools like Hemingway and ProWritingAid assist in maintaining clear, concise, and transparent language in your copy.
5. **Compliance Monitoring:** Tools like AdWords Policy Center ensure your advertising campaigns comply with relevant laws and guidelines.

Conclusion

Ethical copywriting is essential for building trust, maintaining credibility, and fostering long-term relationships with your audience. By adhering to principles of honesty, transparency, and respect, you can create compelling content that not only persuades but also upholds your brand's integrity. In the next chapter, we will explore the use of urgency and scarcity in copywriting and how to use these techniques ethically.

Chapter 18: The Psychology of Color in Copywriting

Why Color Matters

Color plays a significant role in influencing human emotions, perceptions, and behaviors. In copywriting, understanding the psychology of color can help you create more effective and persuasive content. By strategically using colors, you can evoke specific emotions, enhance brand recognition, and guide your audience's actions.

The Psychological Effects of Colors

1. **Red:** Conveys energy, urgency, and passion. It can create a sense of excitement and encourage action, making it effective for calls to action (CTAs).
2. **Blue:** Evokes trust, calmness, and reliability. It is commonly used by financial institutions and healthcare brands to convey stability and professionalism.
3. **Green:** Associated with growth, health, and tranquility. It is often used in environmental and wellness brands.
4. **Yellow:** Represents happiness, optimism, and attention. It can be used to create a sense of positivity and highlight important information.
5. **Orange:** Combines the energy of red and the

cheerfulness of yellow. It is often used to create a sense of enthusiasm and encourage impulse actions.

6. **Purple:** Conveys luxury, creativity, and wisdom. It is often used by brands targeting a high-end or creative audience.
7. **Black:** Represents sophistication, elegance, and power. It is commonly used in luxury and high-end brands.
8. **White:** Symbolizes purity, simplicity, and cleanliness. It is often used to create a sense of space and minimalism.
9. **Gray:** Conveys neutrality, balance, and sophistication. It is often used in combination with other colors to create a modern look.

How to Use Color Effectively in Copywriting

1. **Match Brand Identity:** Choose colors that align with your brand's identity and values. Consistent use of brand colors helps in building recognition and trust.
2. **Evoke Desired Emotions:** Use colors strategically to evoke the emotions you want your audience to feel. For example, use blue for trust and green for health.
3. **Guide Attention:** Use contrasting colors to highlight important elements, such as CTAs, headlines, or key information.
4. **Ensure Readability:** Ensure that text colors contrast well with the background to maintain readability. Avoid color combinations that strain the eyes.
5. **Create Visual Hierarchy:** Use different colors to create a visual hierarchy and guide the reader's eye through the content.

Practical Examples of Color Usage

- **CTA Buttons:** Use bold, contrasting colors like red or orange for CTA buttons to make them stand out and encourage clicks.

- **Headlines and Subheadings:** Use a different color for headlines and subheadings to create a clear structure and highlight key points.
- **Background Colors:** Use subtle background colors to create a specific mood or draw attention to certain sections without overwhelming the reader.
- **Product Pages:** Use color to differentiate product categories and highlight special offers or discounts.

Best Practices for Using Color

1. **Test and Optimize:** Conduct A/B testing to see which color combinations resonate best with your audience and drive desired actions.
2. **Consider Cultural Differences:** Be aware that color perceptions can vary across different cultures. Research and adapt your color choices for a global audience.
3. **Maintain Consistency:** Use a consistent color palette across all marketing materials to strengthen brand recognition.
4. **Use Color Psychology Wisely:** Understand the psychological impact of colors and use them purposefully to enhance your messaging.
5. **Avoid Overuse:** Don't use too many colors at once. Stick to a cohesive color scheme to avoid visual clutter and maintain a professional appearance.

Tools for Choosing and Implementing Colors

1. **Color Palettes:** Tools like Adobe Color, Coolors, and Paletton help you create and test color palettes.
2. **Design Software:** Programs like Adobe Photoshop, Illustrator, and Canva offer extensive color options and tools for implementing your color scheme.
3. **Accessibility Checkers:** Tools like Contrast Checker and Color Safe ensure your color combinations are

accessible to all users.

4. **Brand Guidelines:** Develop a brand style guide that includes your color palette and guidelines for its use across different mediums.

Conclusion

The psychology of color is a powerful tool in copywriting that can influence your audience's emotions, perceptions, and behaviors. By understanding and strategically using colors, you can create more effective, engaging, and persuasive content. In the next chapter, we will explore the importance of typography in copywriting and how to use fonts and typefaces to enhance readability and convey your message effectively.

Chapter 19: The Importance of Typography in Copywriting

Why Typography Matters

Typography is a critical element in copywriting that affects readability, aesthetics, and the overall user experience. The right choice of fonts and typefaces can enhance your content's clarity, emphasize key points, and convey your brand's personality. Understanding typography helps you create visually appealing and easily readable content that engages and retains your audience.

The Elements of Typography

1. **Typeface and Font:** The typeface is the design of the lettering (e.g., Arial, Times New Roman), while the font is the specific style within that typeface (e.g., Arial Bold, Times New Roman Italic).
2. **Font Size:** The size of the text, which impacts readability. Larger sizes are generally used for headings, while smaller sizes are used for body text.
3. **Line Spacing (Leading):** The vertical space between lines of text. Proper line spacing improves readability and reduces eye strain.
4. **Letter Spacing (Tracking):** The horizontal space between characters in a block of text. Adjusting tracking can affect the text's readability and aesthetic

appeal.

5. **Line Length:** The width of a block of text. Optimal line length improves readability by making text easier to follow.

6. **Alignment:** The arrangement of text within a page or a section (e.g., left-aligned, center-aligned, justified). Proper alignment helps guide the reader's eye and creates a clean, professional appearance.

How to Use Typography Effectively

1. **Choose Readable Fonts:** Select fonts that are easy to read, especially for body text. Avoid overly decorative or complex fonts for large blocks of text.

2. **Maintain Consistency:** Use a consistent set of fonts throughout your content to create a cohesive look. Typically, this means one font for headings and another for body text.

3. **Use Hierarchy:** Create a clear typographic hierarchy by varying font sizes and weights for headings, subheadings, and body text. This guides the reader's eye and highlights important information.

4. **Optimize Line Spacing:** Ensure adequate line spacing to improve readability. Too little space can make text feel cramped, while too much space can disrupt the reading flow.

5. **Limit Line Length:** Aim for 50-75 characters per line to maintain optimal readability. Lines that are too long or too short can be challenging to read.

6. **Align Text Properly:** Use left alignment for most body text, as it is the easiest to read. Center and right alignment can be used for headings or special sections.

Practical Examples of Typography in Copywriting

- **Headings and Subheadings:** Use larger, bold fonts to differentiate headings and subheadings from body text. This creates a clear structure and helps readers navigate the content.

- **Body Text:** Use a readable, sans-serif font like Arial or Helvetica for body text. Ensure the font size is comfortable to read on all devices.
- **Quotes and Highlights:** Use italic or bold styles to emphasize quotes, key points, or important information.
- **Call-to-Action (CTA):** Use a bold, eye-catching font for CTAs to draw attention and encourage clicks.

Best Practices for Using Typography

1. **Test Readability:** Regularly test your typography on different devices and screen sizes to ensure readability and a consistent user experience.
2. **Use Web-Safe Fonts:** Choose web-safe fonts that are widely supported across different browsers and devices.
3. **Avoid Excessive Fonts:** Limit the number of different fonts to two or three to maintain a clean and professional appearance.
4. **Consider Accessibility:** Ensure your typography choices are accessible to all users, including those with visual impairments. Use sufficient contrast between text and background colors.
5. **Stay Updated:** Keep up with typographic trends and best practices to ensure your content remains modern and visually appealing.

Tools for Typography

1. **Font Libraries:** Google Fonts, Adobe Fonts, and Typekit offer a wide range of fonts for different styles and purposes.
2. **Typography Tools:** Tools like Fontjoy and Type Genius help you pair fonts effectively and create harmonious

typographic designs.
3. **Design Software:** Adobe Illustrator, InDesign, and Canva provide advanced typography tools for creating custom designs.
4. **Accessibility Checkers:** Tools like WAVE and Color Contrast Analyzer ensure your typography choices are accessible and readable for all users.

Conclusion

Typography is a vital aspect of copywriting that influences readability, aesthetics, and the overall user experience. By choosing the right fonts, maintaining consistency, and optimizing typographic elements, you can enhance your content's effectiveness and appeal. In the next chapter, we will explore the role of layout and design in copywriting and how to create visually appealing and effective content layouts.

Chapter 20: The Role of Layout and Design in Copywriting

Why Layout and Design Matter

The layout and design of your content significantly impact its readability, engagement, and overall effectiveness. A well-structured layout guides the reader's eye, highlights important information, and creates a visually appealing experience. Understanding the principles of layout and design helps you create content that is both aesthetically pleasing and easy to navigate.

Key Principles of Layout and Design

1. **Balance:** Distribute elements evenly to create a sense of stability and harmony. Balance can be symmetrical (elements are mirrored on either side) or asymmetrical (different elements are balanced by visual weight).

2. **Contrast:** Use contrast to highlight important elements and create visual interest. Contrast can be achieved through color, size, shape, and typography.

3. **Alignment:** Ensure that elements are properly aligned to create a clean and organized appearance. Consistent alignment helps guide the reader's eye through the content.

4. **Proximity:** Group related elements together to create a cohesive and organized layout. Proximity helps readers

understand the relationship between different pieces of information.

5. **Repetition:** Use repeating elements to create consistency and reinforce your brand identity. Repetition of colors, fonts, and design elements helps unify your content.

6. **White Space:** Use white space (or negative space) to give your content room to breathe. White space improves readability and allows key elements to stand out.

How to Use Layout and Design Effectively

1. **Create a Visual Hierarchy:** Establish a clear visual hierarchy to guide readers through your content. Use headings, subheadings, and varying font sizes to differentiate between sections and highlight important information.

2. **Use Grids:** Utilize grid systems to structure your layout and ensure consistency. Grids help align elements and create a balanced, professional appearance.

3. **Incorporate Visuals:** Use images, infographics, and icons to break up text and add visual interest. Ensure that visuals complement the content and reinforce your message.

4. **Prioritize Readability:** Choose fonts, colors, and layouts that enhance readability. Avoid cluttered designs and ensure sufficient contrast between text and background.

5. **Design for Mobile:** Ensure your layout is responsive and looks good on all devices, including mobile phones and tablets. Test your design on different screen sizes to maintain a consistent user experience.

6. **Highlight CTAs:** Make calls-to-action (CTAs) stand out by using contrasting colors, bold fonts, and strategic

placement. Ensure CTAs are easy to find and encourage clicks.

Practical Examples of Layout and Design in Copywriting

- **Blog Posts:** Use a clear structure with headings, subheadings, and bullet points to break up text and improve readability. Incorporate images and infographics to illustrate key points.
- **Landing Pages:** Use a grid layout to organize content and create a visual hierarchy. Highlight CTAs with contrasting colors and ensure important information is above the fold.
- **Email Newsletters:** Use a clean and organized layout with clear headings, sections, and CTAs. Include visuals to make the content more engaging and break up long blocks of text.
- **Product Pages:** Use a grid layout to display product images, descriptions, and CTAs. Highlight key features and benefits with bullet points and use white space to avoid clutter.

Best Practices for Layout and Design

1. **Test and Iterate:** Continuously test different layouts and designs to see what works best for your audience. Use A/B testing to compare different versions and gather insights.
2. **Follow Design Trends:** Stay updated with current design trends and best practices to ensure your content remains modern and visually appealing.
3. **Maintain Consistency:** Use consistent layouts, colors, and fonts across all marketing materials to create a cohesive brand experience.
4. **Gather Feedback:** Seek feedback from users and stakeholders to identify areas for improvement and ensure your design meets their needs and preferences.

5. **Use Professional Tools:** Utilize professional design tools and software to create high-quality layouts and designs.

Tools for Layout and Design

1. **Design Software:** Adobe Illustrator, InDesign, and Canva offer advanced tools for creating custom layouts and designs.
2. **Website Builders:** Platforms like WordPress, Squarespace, and Wix provide templates and tools for designing responsive websites.
3. **Email Marketing Tools:** Mailchimp, Constant Contact, and Campaign Monitor offer templates and design tools for creating email newsletters.
4. **A/B Testing Tools:** Optimizely, VWO, and Google Optimize help you test and compare different layouts and designs.
5. **Grid Systems:** Bootstrap, Foundation, and Grid by Example offer grid systems for creating structured and responsive layouts.

Conclusion

Layout and design are essential components of effective copywriting. By understanding and applying key design principles, you can create visually appealing, readable, and engaging content. In the next chapter, we will explore the use of white space in copywriting and how to use it effectively to enhance readability and focus.

Chapter 21: The Use of White Space in Copywriting

Why White Space Matters

White space, also known as negative space, is the empty space around and between the elements of your design. It plays a crucial role in enhancing readability, reducing visual clutter, and focusing the reader's attention on key elements. Effective use of white space can make your content more appealing and easier to navigate, ultimately improving user experience.

Benefits of White Space

1. **Improves Readability:** White space around text blocks makes the content easier to read and less overwhelming. It helps prevent eye strain and allows readers to process information more effectively.
2. **Enhances Focus:** By isolating important elements, white space draws attention to them. This is particularly useful for highlighting calls-to-action (CTAs), key messages, and important information.
3. **Creates Visual Hierarchy:** White space helps establish a clear visual hierarchy by separating different sections and guiding the reader's eye through the content.
4. **Reduces Clutter:** A clean, uncluttered layout with ample white space creates a sense of order and

professionalism. It helps prevent information overload and makes the content more inviting.

5. **Adds Elegance:** White space can add a sense of sophistication and elegance to your design, enhancing the overall aesthetic appeal.

How to Use White Space Effectively

1. **Break Up Text:** Use white space to separate paragraphs, headings, and sections. This creates a clear structure and makes the content more digestible.

2. **Isolate Key Elements:** Surround important elements, such as CTAs, images, and key messages, with white space to make them stand out.

3. **Use Margins and Padding:** Ensure sufficient margins and padding around text blocks, images, and other elements to prevent them from feeling cramped.

4. **Embrace Minimalism:** Adopt a minimalist approach by including only essential elements and allowing ample white space. This reduces visual clutter and enhances focus.

5. **Create Balance:** Distribute white space evenly to create a balanced and harmonious layout. Avoid large empty areas that can create an unbalanced appearance.

Practical Examples of White Space Usage

- **Web Pages:** Use white space to separate different sections, such as the header, body, and footer. Ensure ample space around CTAs and key messages.

- **Blog Posts:** Break up long blocks of text with white space, headings, and images. Use bullet points and lists to create additional white space.

- **Email Newsletters:** Use white space to separate sections, images, and CTAs. Ensure sufficient margins and padding around text blocks.

- **Print Materials:** Use white space in brochures, flyers, and posters to create a clean and professional look. Avoid overcrowding elements.

Best Practices for Using White Space

1. **Prioritize Content:** Focus on the most important content and use white space to highlight it. Avoid filling every inch of space with information.
2. **Test Different Layouts:** Experiment with different layouts and amounts of white space to find the most effective design. Use A/B testing to compare results.
3. **Maintain Consistency:** Use a consistent amount of white space across different sections and pages to create a cohesive look.
4. **Consider Accessibility:** Ensure that your use of white space enhances readability and accessibility for all users, including those with visual impairments.
5. **Stay Updated:** Keep up with design trends and best practices to ensure your use of white space remains modern and effective.

Tools for Optimizing White Space

1. **Design Software:** Adobe InDesign, Illustrator, and Figma offer advanced tools for designing layouts with optimal white space.
2. **Website Builders:** WordPress, Squarespace, and Webflow provide templates and tools for creating clean, white space-friendly websites.
3. **Email Marketing Tools:** Mailchimp, Constant Contact, and Sendinblue offer templates and design options for creating email newsletters with ample white space.
4. **Usability Testing Tools:** UserTesting, Crazy Egg, and Hotjar help you gather feedback and insights on your use of white space.

Conclusion

White space is a powerful tool in copywriting that enhances

readability, reduces clutter, and focuses attention on key elements. By using white space effectively, you can create clean, elegant, and engaging content that improves the overall user experience. In the next chapter, we will delve into the role of images and graphics in copywriting and how to use them to enhance your message.

Chapter 22: The Role of Images and Graphics in Copywriting

Why Images and Graphics Matter

Images and graphics are essential components of effective copywriting. They can capture attention, illustrate complex ideas, evoke emotions, and break up text to make content more engaging. Incorporating visuals strategically can enhance your message, improve comprehension, and make your content more memorable.

Benefits of Using Images and Graphics

1. **Captures Attention:** Visuals are more likely to grab the reader's attention than text alone, making them crucial for drawing readers into your content.
2. **Enhances Understanding:** Images and graphics can simplify complex information, making it easier for readers to understand and retain key points.
3. **Elicits Emotion:** Visuals can evoke emotions and create a deeper connection with your audience, reinforcing your message and encouraging engagement.
4. **Breaks Up Text:** Incorporating images and graphics breaks up long blocks of text, making your content more readable and less intimidating.
5. **Improves Retention:** People are more likely to

remember information presented visually, enhancing the overall impact of your content.

Types of Visual Elements

1. **Photographs:** High-quality photos that complement your text and provide a visual representation of your message.
2. **Illustrations:** Custom drawings or designs that can add a unique and creative touch to your content.
3. **Infographics:** Visual representations of data and information that make complex concepts easier to understand.
4. **Charts and Graphs:** Tools for displaying data in a clear and concise manner, helping to illustrate key points.
5. **Icons and Symbols:** Simple visuals that can enhance comprehension and guide the reader's eye.
6. **GIFs and Animations:** Dynamic visuals that can add a lively element to your content and capture attention.
7. **Screenshots:** Visuals that provide step-by-step guides or demonstrate features and functionality.

How to Use Images and Graphics Effectively

1. **Align with Your Message:** Ensure your visuals are relevant to your content and reinforce your message. They should add value, not distract.
2. **Use High-Quality Visuals:** Select clear, high-resolution images and graphics. Avoid generic stock photos that don't add meaningful context.
3. **Keep It Simple:** Avoid cluttering your content with too many visuals. Use them strategically to enhance, not overwhelm.
4. **Ensure Consistency:** Maintain a consistent style and color scheme for all visuals to create a cohesive look.
5. **Optimize for Speed:** Compress images and optimize

graphics to ensure fast loading times, which is crucial for user experience and SEO.

6. **Include Alt Text:** Add descriptive alt text to all images for accessibility and SEO purposes.

Practical Examples of Visual Elements in Copywriting

- **Blog Posts:** Use images, infographics, and pull quotes to break up text and illustrate key points.
- **Product Pages:** Include high-quality product photos, demo videos, and customer review snippets to enhance the product description.
- **Landing Pages:** Use a combination of images, icons, and videos to highlight benefits, features, and calls to action.
- **Email Newsletters:** Incorporate visuals like GIFs, charts, and banners to make your emails more engaging and visually appealing.
- **Social Media Posts:** Use eye-catching images, infographics, and short videos to capture attention and drive engagement.

Best Practices for Using Images and Graphics

1. **Prioritize Relevance:** Ensure every visual element serves a purpose and aligns with your content's message.
2. **Use Captions:** Add captions to images and videos to provide context and enhance understanding.
3. **Optimize for Mobile:** Ensure your visuals are responsive and look good on all devices, including mobile phones and tablets.
4. **A/B Test Visuals:** Test different visual elements to see which ones resonate best with your audience and drive the desired actions.
5. **Leverage User-Generated Content:** Encourage customers to share their photos and videos of your

product, adding authenticity and social proof.

Tools for Creating and Optimizing Visual Elements

1. **Graphic Design Tools:** Canva, Adobe Spark, and Piktochart for creating images, infographics, and social media graphics.
2. **Video Creation Tools:** Animoto, WeVideo, and Adobe Premiere Rush for creating and editing videos.
3. **Image Optimization Tools:** TinyPNG, ImageOptim, and Compressor.io for compressing images without losing quality.
4. **Screen Capture Tools:** Snagit, Lightshot, and Greenshot for taking and editing screenshots.
5. **Stock Photo Resources:** Unsplash, Pexels, and Shutterstock for finding high-quality, royalty-free images.

Conclusion

Incorporating images and graphics into your copywriting is essential for creating engaging, memorable, and effective content. By using visuals strategically, you can enhance your message, improve comprehension, and drive better results. In the next chapter, we will explore the role of storytelling in copywriting and how to craft compelling narratives that captivate your audience.

Chapter 23: The Art of Writing Persuasive Headlines

Why Headlines Matter

Headlines are the first thing readers see, and they play a crucial role in capturing attention and encouraging further reading. A compelling headline can make the difference between a reader engaging with your content or moving on to something else. Understanding how to craft persuasive headlines is essential for effective copywriting.

Key Elements of a Persuasive Headline

1. **Clarity:** Your headline should be clear and easily understood. Avoid ambiguity and ensure the reader knows what to expect.
2. **Relevance:** The headline must be relevant to the target audience and address their needs, interests, or pain points.
3. **Urgency:** Creating a sense of urgency can encourage readers to act immediately. Use time-sensitive words and phrases to convey this urgency.
4. **Curiosity:** A headline that piques curiosity can entice readers to click and learn more. However, be careful not to use misleading or clickbait tactics.
5. **Benefit-Oriented:** Highlight the benefits or value the reader will gain from reading the content. Focus on

what's in it for them.

6. **Emotion:** Emotional triggers can make your headline more compelling. Use words that evoke emotions such as excitement, fear, joy, or surprise.

Types of Persuasive Headlines

1. **How-To Headlines:** These provide a clear benefit by offering a solution or guide. Example: "How to Boost Your Productivity in Just One Week."

2. **List Headlines:** These headlines promise a list of items, making the content easy to digest. Example: "10 Proven Strategies to Increase Your Sales."

3. **Question Headlines:** Asking a question can to engage the reader's curiosity and encourage them to find the answer. Example: "Are You Making These Common Marketing Mistakes?"

4. **Command Headlines:** Directly tell the reader what to do, creating a sense of urgency. Example: "Get Your Free E-Book Today!"

5. **Comparison Headlines:** Compare two or more options to highlight benefits. Example: "SEO vs. PPC: Which Is Right for Your Business?"

6. **Testimonial Headlines:** Use customer testimonials to build credibility and trust. Example: "See Why Our Clients Call Us the Best in the Business."

7. **News Headlines:** Share news or updates relevant to your audience. Example: "Introducing Our Latest Feature to Streamline Your Workflow."

How to Craft Persuasive Headlines

1. **Know Your Audience:** Understand your audience's needs, interests, and pain points. Tailor your headlines to resonate with them.

2. **Use Power Words:** Incorporate words that evoke emotions and drive action, such as "free," "exclusive,"

"proven," and "ultimate."

3. **Keep It Short and Sweet:** Aim for concise headlines that are easy to read and understand. Ideally, keep your headlines under 70 characters.
4. **Test Different Headlines:** Experiment with different headline variations to see which ones perform best. Use A/B testing to gather insights.
5. **Use Numbers:** Numbers can make your headline more specific and appealing. For example, "7 Tips for Better Sleep" is more engaging than "Tips for Better Sleep."
6. **Incorporate Keywords:** Use relevant keywords to improve SEO and help your headline rank higher in search results.

Practical Examples of Persuasive Headlines

- **For a Blog Post:** "5 Simple Steps to Improve Your Website's SEO"
- **For a Product Page:** "Discover the Ultimate Solution for Back Pain Relief"
- **For an Email Newsletter:** "Unlock Exclusive Discounts with Our VIP Membership"
- **For a Social Media Post:** "Is Your Marketing Strategy Ready for 2024? Find Out Now!"
- **For a Landing Page:** "Get Started with Our Free 30-Day Trial Today!"

Best Practices for Writing Headlines

1. **Be Specific:** Provide clear and specific information about what the reader will gain from your content.
2. **Avoid Clickbait:** Ensure your headline accurately represents the content. Misleading headlines can damage trust and credibility.
3. **Leverage Data:** Use statistics or data points to make your headline more compelling and credible.

4. **Create a Sense of Scarcity:** Phrases like "limited time offer" or "only a few spots left" can encourage readers to act quickly.
5. **Revise and Refine:** Don't settle for the first headline you write. Take the time to revise and refine it for maximum impact.

Tools for Crafting Headlines

1. **Headline Analyzers:** Tools like CoSchedule's Headline Analyzer and Sharethrough Headline Analyzer can help you assess the effectiveness of your headlines.
2. **A/B Testing Tools:** Platforms like Optimizely and VWO allow you to test different headlines to see which ones perform best.
3. **Keyword Research Tools:** Use tools like Google Keyword Planner, Ahrefs, and SEMrush to find relevant keywords for your headlines.
4. **Thesaurus and Synonym Finders:** Tools like Thesaurus.com can help you find powerful and varied words to enhance your headlines.

Conclusion

Writing persuasive headlines is an art that requires a deep understanding of your audience, a clear and compelling message, and strategic use of language. By crafting headlines that capture attention and encourage engagement, you can significantly increase the effectiveness of your copy. In the next chapter, we will explore the importance of the call-to-action (CTA) in copywriting and how to create CTAs that drive results.

www.ingramcontent.com/pod-product-compliance
Lightning Source LLC
Chambersburg PA
CBHW071946210526
45479CB00002B/837